Library of Congress Cataloging-in-Publication Data

Penner, Lucille Recht. The tea party book / by Lucille Recht Penner; illustrated
by Jody Wheeler   p. cm.

Summary: Includes easy recipes and instructions for decorations, favors, and
simple activities for all kinds of tea parties.

ISBN 0-679-82440-5 (trade) — ISBN 0-679-92440-X (lib. bdg.)

1. Children's parties—Juvenile literature.   2. Cookery—Juvenile literature.   3. Party
decorations—Juvenile literature.   [1. Afternoon teas. 2. Parties. 3. Cookery.]
I. Wheeler, Jody, ill. II. Title   TX 731.P37 1993   793.2'1-dc20   91-52903

Manufactured in the United States of America

3   4   5   6   7   8   9   10

The Tea Party Book

written *by* LUCILLE RECHT PENNER
illustrated *by* JODY WHEELER

with menus, recipes, decorations,
and favors to make

RANDOM HOUSE 🏠 NEW YORK

Polly, put the kettle on,
Polly, put the kettle on,
Polly, put the kettle on,
And we'll all have tea.

 Contents

Making Tea

You can serve any drink you like at a tea party—apple juice, milk, lemonade, cocoa—as long as you serve it in pretty teacups. If you don't want regular tea, which has caffeine in it, there are lots of other teas you can make, too—fruit teas like lemon or apple or peach, spicy teas like cinnamon or peppermint, and teas with their own special tastes like almond or licorice.

You can make all these different teas in the same way. To prepare tea for four people, put two bags in the pot. Ask an adult to help you pour four cups of boiling water over the tea bags. (You can double or triple this recipe if you have lots of guests and a big teapot.)

Wait five minutes. Then (with an adult's help) pour the hot tea into cups. Remember to ask your guests whether they'd like milk or sugar or lemon slices.

SPECIAL NOTE Always be sure an adult helps you when you work with boiling water, hot stoves, knives, or scissors.

WHERE DOES TEA COME FROM?

Tea is made from the leaves of a special kind of evergreen plant. The Chinese discovered what a good-tasting drink it made almost 5,000 years ago. Back then they used monkeys to pick the tea leaves!

Fancy Cakes
and Little Sandwiches

Making tea party treats is as much fun as eating them. You can use your imagination to create dainty sandwiches, pretty little cakes, and decorations you can eat!

Tea sandwiches can be squares or triangles or strips or rounds—but they *never* have crusts! (Use any filling you like.) Dress up a sandwich with a carrot curl or a bit of red pepper.

Make a cookie special by dipping a corner in melted chocolate. And this is a wonderful trick: Put a stencil on a cookie or a slice of cake. (If you don't have a stencil, cut a heart or another simple shape from a piece of paper.) Sprinkle powdered sugar on it, take the stencil away, and you'll have a delicious design!

For a pretty little cake, cut out a round of angel food cake with a cookie cutter. Spread it with whipped cream, and put a slice of banana on top. Presto!—you have banana cream cake. (With a strawberry, this is strawberry shortcake!) Make a triple layer cake with three rounds of pound cake. Put icing between the layers, and ice the top. Put a jelly bean in the center of each cake.

A Teddy Bear Tea Party

Teddy bear, Teddy bear, I love you.

◆ M ◆ E ◆ N ◆ U ◆

TEDDY BEAR COOKIES
BEAR BERRIES AND HONEY BREAD
TEDDY TEA

Your teddy bear is cuddly and lovable. And he's always there when you need him. He's your best friend.

But teddy bears don't get out much. Why not give a tea party for your teddy bear? And surprise him by wearing teddy bear ears! You can serve your teddy bear his favorite foods—berries and honey. And give him special teddy bear cookies for dessert. You might want to invite some friends—and their teddy bears.

TEDDY BEAR COOKIES

Ask an adult to help you make teddy bear cookies.

You will need:

1 stick sweet butter, softened	*¹/₄ cup cocoa*
¹/₂ cup brown sugar	*¹/₂ teaspoon baking soda*
1 egg	*¹/₂ teaspoon salt*
1 cup flour	*Raisins*

1. Preheat the oven to 350°. Grease a cookie sheet.

2. Cream together butter and brown sugar. Beat in the egg.

3. In a separate bowl, mix the flour, cocoa, baking soda, and salt. Stir this mixture into the butter and sugar. Chill 1 hour or more.

4. Divide the dough into 8 equal pieces. Then divide each piece into 1 large ball (the size of a Ping-Pong ball) for the head and 2 little balls (marble-size) for the ears. Place the balls on the cookie sheet in the shape of a bear face, flatten slightly, and press in the raisins for the eyes and nose. Bake for 15 minutes.

Makes 8 cookies.

BEAR BERRIES AND HONEY BREAD

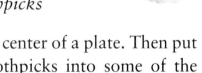

You will need:
Whole-wheat bread   *Honey*
Raspberries or blueberries   *Toothpicks*

1. Put a small bowl of honey in the center of a plate. Then put a circle of berries around it. Stick toothpicks into some of the berries.

2. Cut the crusts off 4 pieces of whole-wheat bread. Then cut each slice into 4 strips. Arrange the strips in a pretty pattern around the bowl of honey and berries.

Here's the secret of Teddy Tea. Serve any tea you like—just put a big spoon of honey in your bear's cup! Turn to page 2 for tea-making directions.

TEDDY BEAR PLACE MATS

You will need: *Colored paper*   *Felt-tip markers*

    Draw little teddy bear faces all over each piece of colored paper. Set one at every place.

TEDDY BEAR EARS

When your guests arrive, everyone can make teddy bear ears.

You will need: *Black felt-tip marker*
Brown colored paper   *Tape*

    1. Cut a circle out of colored paper and cut it in half. Draw a large C on each half. These are the ears.

    2. Cut a strip of colored paper to make a headband. Tape the ends together. Then tape on the ears. You're all finished!

As soon as it's time to eat, put on your teddy bear ears. Dip the bread and berries in the honey. And don't forget the cookies!

A Valentine Tea

Will you be my valentine?

MENU

HAVE-A-HEART SANDWICHES
PINK PUDDING
PINK TEA

Some people give chocolates for Valentine's Day. Some give roses. But you can give your favorite people a beautiful Valentine Tea! Decorate the table with flowers, hearts, and ribbons. Then bring out heart-shaped sandwiches and pink pudding, and pour out pink tea. It might be fun to make valentines together, too. Happy Valentine's Day!

PINK PUDDING

You will need:
1 small package red Jell-O

1 cup vanilla yogurt
Thin pink ribbon

Ask an adult to help you. Boil one cup of water. Pour water and Jell-O into a bowl. Mix well and cool. Stir in the yogurt. Pour it into small cups. Now refrigerate overnight. When you are ready to serve the pudding, take out the cups and tie a pink ribbon around each cup.

9

HAVE-A-HEART
SANDWICHES

You will need:
Heart-shaped cookie cutter
Whole-wheat bread

White bread
Strawberries
Cream cheese, softened

1. Use the cookie cutter to cut hearts out of the bread.

2. Wash the berries and mash them into the cream cheese with a fork. It's okay if the berries are lumpy.

3. Spread a white-bread heart with strawberry cream cheese. Top it with a whole-wheat-bread heart. Make two sandwiches for each guest. Serve on a pretty plate with a few strawberries.

For Pink Tea, try rose hips or strawberry teas. Or fill a teapot halfway with cranberry juice, and add hot water. Turn to page 2 for tea-making directions and more ideas.

VALENTINE MENUS

Make a pretty valentine menu for each guest!

You will need:
Red colored paper
A felt-tip marker

Tape
Popsicle sticks
Pink ribbon

Cut each sheet of red paper into 4 pieces. Cut hearts out of the pieces—one for each guest. Write on each heart:

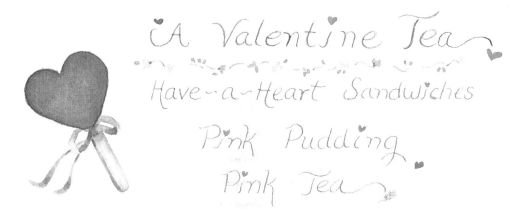

A Valentine Tea

Have-a-Heart Sandwiches

Pink Pudding

Pink Tea

Tape Popsicle sticks to the backs of the menus. Tie a pink ribbon bow onto the stick. When you set the table, put a menu next to each plate.

It may be hard to say goodbye after such a beautiful tea party. But if each guest takes a menu home, they'll always remember having a Valentine Tea with you.

Tea by the Sea

By the sea, by the sea,
by the beautiful sea . . .

· M · E · N · U ·

BITE-SIZE HOT DOGS IN TORTILLAS
SAND BARS
TEAPOT LEMONADE

There's nothing like the beach. The sea breezes rippling your hair . . . the sand between your toes . . . the splashing of the waves . . . a delicious picnic lunch . . .

You don't have to wait for summer to have a Tea by the Sea Party!

BITE-SIZE HOT DOGS IN TORTILLAS

What would you like to eat by the sea?
Hot dogs, and plenty of them!

You will need: *Toothpicks*
Hot dogs   *Ketchup*
Flour tortillas   *Mustard*

Ask an adult to help with this recipe. Preheat the oven to 350°F. Cut each hot dog into 3 pieces. Cut each tortilla into 3 long strips. Wrap the strips around the hot-dog pieces. Fasten them with toothpicks and place on a cookie sheet. Bake in the oven for 5 minutes. Your guests can give their hot dogs a quick dip—in small bowls of ketchup and mustard, of course!

SAND BARS

You will need:
½ gallon ice cream

1 package vanilla wafers
8 x 8 pan

Let the ice cream soften and spread it evenly throughout the pan. Put the cookies in a plastic bag and gently pound them until they are finely crushed. Sprinkle the cookie "sand" over the top of the ice cream and freeze for 2 hours. Cut into squares and serve!

Fill the teapot with lemonade. Before serving, put a slice of lemon in each teacup.

 ## SEASHORE CENTERPIECE

You will need:
Colored paper
A clear glass pie plate
Double-stick tape

Felt-tip markers
Yellow Play-Doh
Sea shells or pebbles

1. Cut out a long strip of blue paper. Make scallops along one edge. Tape it around the outside of the pie plate.
2. Cut 3 or 4 little fish from colored paper. Use markers to give them stripes, spots, eyes, and fins. Tape the fish on the paper.

3. Put a thin layer of yellow Play-Doh in the plate to look like sand. Scatter some sea shells or little pebbles on the sand. If you like, make a Play-Doh sandcastle in the middle.

OCEAN WAVE PLACE CARDS

Make place cards that look like this:

You're all ready for your Tea by the Sea Party! If your fingers are sticky after you eat, just pass around bowls of salt water to clean them. You may even want to fill the bathtub with warm water and bubbles and take a dip after tea.

A Japanese Tea Party

• M • E • N • U •

NOODLE SOUP
SWEET RICE CAKES
GREEN TEA

When the doorbell rings, open the door, bow, and say, "*Konichi wa.*" That means "Good afternoon" in Japanese.

Now ask your friends to take off their shoes. At a Japanese Tea Party you're supposed to drink tea wearing your socks!

Decorate a branch with tissue-paper cherry blossoms for a centerpiece. Put your prettiest teacups on a low coffee table. You can sit around the table on the floor, Japanese-style, at this tea party. Did you know that "tea" in Japanese is *o cha*?

NOODLE SOUP

Everyone likes noodle soup. And it's easy to make.

You will need: *1 package Japanese-style noodle soup*

Ask an adult to help you make the soup. Just follow the directions on the package. Spoon soup into small bowls and serve.

In Japan people drink lots of green tea. Make it according to the directions on page 2.

• 17 •

SWEET RICE CAKES

You will need: *1 package rice cakes* *Honey*

Spread the rice cakes with a thin layer of honey. Place them on a cookie sheet. Set aside. When you're ready to eat, ask an adult to help you put the cakes under the broiler for one minute. Serve warm.

CHERRY BLOSSOM CENTERPIECE

You will need: *Pink tissue paper*
A small branch *Pipe cleaners*

Find a small branch and strip off the leaves. To make each blossom, cut an 8-inch square of pink tissue paper. Gently crumple the square of paper. Twist one end of a pipe cleaner around the middle of the crumpled paper. Twist the other end around the tree branch. Make three or four cherry blossoms for the branch.

JAPANESE FANS

Make some cherry-blossom-and-butterfly fans!

You will need: *Colored paper*
Felt-tip markers   *Tape*

Draw pictures of cherry blossoms and butterflies on one side of the colored paper. Starting at the short edge, fold the paper accordion style. When the paper is all folded up, tape one end closed for the handle. Fan out the other end. Make enough fans for everyone.

When it's time to say goodbye, help your guests find their shoes.

But don't say "goodbye" in English. Say it in Japanese: "*Sayonara.*"

A Royal Tea Party

Lavender blue, dilly dilly,
Lavender green,
When I am king, dilly dilly,
you shall be queen.

◆ M ◆ E ◆ N ◆ U ◆

ROYAL TRIFLE
CUCUMBER SANDWICHES
GOLDEN TEA

Make way . . . Royal guests are coming to tea! Your guests will feel like kings and queens with thrones to sit on, glittering scepters to wave, and lots of royal goodies to eat. Don't forget to dress up and wear your fanciest jewelry at this tea party!

ROYAL TRIFLE

A trifle is very special. Use a pretty, clear bowl so everyone can see the layers of pudding, jam, cake, and whipped cream.

You will need:
Ladyfingers
A glass bowl
Orange juice

Strawberry jam
1 small package instant vanilla
* pudding*
Whipping cream

1. Arrange a layer of ladyfingers in the bottom of the glass bowl. Sprinkle some orange juice on the ladyfingers. Spread a thin layer of jam on top.

2. Make the vanilla pudding according to the package directions. Spoon one-third of it over the jam.

3. Add two more layers of ladyfingers, juice, jam, and pudding. Ask an adult to help you whip the cream. Spread it on top.

CUCUMBER SANDWICHES

Make a lot of these tiny cucumber sandwiches. They taste great!

You will need:
Vegetable peeler   *Whole-wheat bread*
Cucumbers   *Cream cheese, softened*

1. Ask an adult to help you peel the cucumbers and cut them into thin slices.

2. Cut the crusts off the bread. Spread cream cheese on each slice of bread. Arrange a thin layer of cucumbers on one slice. Top with another slice. Press gently. Then cut the sandwich into four triangles. Arrange the cucumber sandwiches on a platter.

For Golden Tea, follow the tea-making directions on page 2. Then add two drops of yellow food coloring to the pot. Presto! Glorious Golden Tea!

ROYAL THRONES

Your royal guests will need thrones to sit on. Put two fluffy cushions or pillows on each chair, and there they are—instant thrones!

ROYAL NAME CARDS

Make place cards that look like this:

ROYAL SCEPTERS

Kings and queens love to wave their scepters. Make some for your guests in case they forget their own.

You will need: *Colored paper   Glitter paste   Tape   A glass*

Roll a piece of colored paper the long way into a tube. Tape the edge so it won't unroll. Paint half of the tube with glitter paste. Stick it in a glass to dry. When it's dry, turn it upside down and paint the other half.

Put a name card and a scepter on each plate. Invite everyone to take a throne. Then bring out the Royal Trifle.

Ta-da! What a dish to set before a king and queen!

Be sure to stand at the door when your guests leave. Take a bow. You deserve it. That was a tea party fit for a king and queen!

A Full-Moon Tea Party

What's the news of the day,
Good neighbor, I pray?
They say a balloon
Has gone up to the moon!

◆ M ◆ E ◆ N ◆ U ◆

MOON SCONES
CHEESE STARS AND APPLE CRESCENTS
MILKY WAY TEA

It's wintertime and night falls early. A full moon is shining. So turn the lights down low, put a table by a window—and have a moonlight tea party! You can serve moon scones, cheese stars, and apple crescents on place mats decorated with moons and stars. You can even have your own moon centerpiece! Just hang a big yellow balloon from the ceiling. And remember to look at the moon through your party favors—homemade telescopes!

MOON SCONES

Ask an adult to help you make moon scones.

You will need:
1 ¹/₂ cups flour
¹/₂ stick sweet butter, softened

¹/₃ cup sugar
¹/₂ cup milk
¹/₃ cup golden raisins

1. Preheat oven to 425°.

2. Put the flour and butter in a big bowl. Cut the butter into pieces. Then use your fingers to rub the butter and flour together until the mixture looks like crumbs. Mix in the sugar. Add the milk and mix well. Gently stir in the raisins.

3. Chill the dough for 1 hour or more. Shape it into Ping-Pong-size balls. Put them on a greased cookie sheet, flatten them, and bake 12 to 15 minutes. Serve warm with jam or honey.

Makes 12 scones.

CHEESE STARS AND APPLE CRESCENTS

You will need:
A star-shaped cookie cutter

Cheese slices
Apples

Cut the stars out of the cheese slices with the cookie cutter. Ask an adult to help you cut apple slices. Arrange your stars and apple crescents on a pretty plate.

To make Milky Way Tea, stir together 1 teaspoon honey, $\frac{1}{4}$ teaspoon vanilla, and 1 cup milk for each person. Ask an adult to help you warm the mixture in a saucepan and pour it into a teapot.

NIGHT SKY PLACE MATS

You can make place mats that glitter like the night sky!

You will need:
Aluminum foil
Glue

Black colored paper
Gold star stickers

Cut small round moons out of the foil. Glue the moons onto pieces of black colored paper. Stick on some gold star stickers.

TELESCOPES

Everyone will love having a homemade telescope party favor.

You will need:
Black colored paper   Plastic wrap
Tape   Silver star stickers

1. To make each telescope, cut a piece of black paper in half. Roll the paper into a tube and tape it together. Cut a circle out of plastic wrap. Tape it over one end of the paper tube.

2. Stick some silver stars on the plastic wrap. Everyone can look at the yellow "moon" balloon through their telescopes. They can use them to look at the real moon too.

All set? Ask an adult to take pictures of you and your friends around the yellow balloon moon.

Say "Cheese."

A Garden Tea Party

She loves me, she loves me not . . .

◆ M ◆ E ◆ N ◆ U ◆

PINWHEEL SANDWICHES
ICE-CREAM FLOWER SUNDAES
ICED TEA

The sun is shining in a blue sky. Birds are singing. The flowers are in bloom and a soft breeze sends their fragrance everywhere.

What could be lovelier than a tea party out in the garden?

On a nice warm day, set up a table on the lawn. Decorate it with flowers, of course. For an extra-special centerpiece, float some blossoms in a clear bowl of water.

Bring out a croquet set or put up a badminton net. Your guests can sip tea and nibble on pinwheel sandwiches in between games!

 PINWHEEL SANDWICHES

These little sandwiches are very pretty!

You will need:
Rolling pin   *Peanut butter (or any filling*
White bread   *you like)*

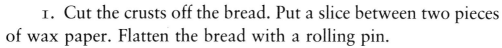

1. Cut the crusts off the bread. Put a slice between two pieces of wax paper. Flatten the bread with a rolling pin.

2. Peel the paper away. Spread the bread with peanut butter. Gently roll up the slice of bread into the shape of a log. Slice into rounds. Arrange your pinwheels on a plate in a flower shape.

ICE-CREAM FLOWER SUNDAES

Your guests will love making their own ice-cream flower sundaes.

You will need:
Scoops of vanilla ice cream   *Chopped walnuts*
Peaches, berries   *Sunflower seeds*

1. Put scoops of vanilla ice cream (one for each guest) on a cookie sheet lined with waxed paper. Freeze them for one hour or longer.

2. Wash the berries and the peaches. Ask an adult to help you cut the peaches into slices. Put the fruit, chopped walnuts, and sunflower seeds into separate bowls. Put spoons in each bowl.

3. When you are ready to eat, put a scoop of ice cream on a dessert plate for each guest. Your guests can make their own flower sundaes.

To make Iced Tea, follow the tea-making directions on page 2, but put one extra tea bag in the pot. Let the tea cool. Take out the tea bags. Refrigerate for at least one hour or until it's time for the party.

PETAL PLACE MATS

To dress up the table, make yellow-and-white daisy place mats.

You will need:
White, yellow, and green colored paper   *Glue*

Cut daisy petals out of the white paper. Cut circles out of the yellow paper. Paste a yellow circle in the middle of each piece of green colored paper. Paste the petals around the circle. Make a place mat for each guest.

FLOATING BLOSSOM CENTERPIECE

You will need: *Water*
A clear bowl   *A few blossoms*

Just float a few blossoms in a clear bowl of water.

To set the table, put the bowl of floating blossoms in the center. Arrange the plates of chopped walnuts, sunflower seeds, and peaches around the centerpiece.

When the party's over, give each guest a packet of flower seeds to take home. They can plant them outside or in a big flowerpot. Plant some yourself. Next year these flowers can be the centerpiece for your annual garden tea party!

Tiny Tea

Little drops of water,
Little grains of sand,
Make the mighty ocean
And the pleasant land.

• M • E • N • U •

CHEESE TARTLETS
FROZEN GRAPE POPS
TINY TIDBITS
TINY TEA

Do you love tiny things? Get out your tiniest tea set. Or make one, with thimble cups and button plates! It's time for a Tiny Tea. It's fun to prepare lots of tiny morsels and make tiny books for your guests to take home. Your dolls would enjoy this tea party.

CHEESE TARTLETS

You will need:
Fresh white or oatmeal bread   *Round cookie cutter*
Cheese   *Miniature muffin tin*

1. Ask an adult to help. Preheat the oven to 350°F. Make bread rounds that are a little bigger than the muffin-tin openings. Gently press the bread rounds into the tins until they look like little tarts. (Don't flatten the bread!) Bake 5 minutes.

2. Take the muffin tin from the oven. Fill each tartlet with pieces of cheese. (You can mix with bits of ham or tomato if you like.) Bake 5 minutes more or until cheese is melted. Gently remove from tin. Serve warm.

FROZEN GRAPE POPS

These grape pops will freeze in 30 minutes. Make lots of them!

You will need: *Seedless grapes*   *Toothpicks*

Wash the grapes. Gently pull off the stems. Stick a toothpick into each grape. Put them in the freezer for 30 minutes or longer. Take out the pops when you're ready to serve them.

TINY TIDBITS

Fill miniature paper muffin-tin liners with little treats like chocolate chips, peanuts, raisins, mini-marshmallows, and M&M's. Give one cup to each guest.

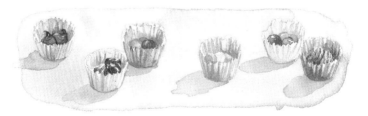

Make your favorite tea and pour it into tiny cups. Just turn to page 2 for tea-making directions.

TINY BOOKS

Tiny books are easy to make.

You will need: *Scraps of cloth*   *White paper*   *A stapler*

1. To make each book, cut out a 2 x 4-inch scrap of cloth. Cut two pieces of white paper the same size as the cloth.

2. Put the scrap of cloth on the table. Lay the two pieces of paper on top of it. Fold in half. Press the fold hard with your thumb.

3. Open the papers. Let an adult help you staple along the fold. Refold. Now you have a tiny book! Make one for each guest. You may want to write a guest's name on each book.

Place the Cheese Tartlets on a plate. When they're gone, serve the Frozen Grape Pops. Now bring out the Tiny Tidbits.

Delicious!

When everyone's finished you can give them their tiny books. They might want to draw some tiny pictures inside—or write down your recipes!

A Rainy-Day Tea Party

Rain, rain, go away,
Come again another day!

٠ M ٠ E ٠ N ٠ U ٠

LEMON DRIZZLE CAKE
CLOUD COOKIES
MUD PIES
RAINY-DAY TEA

It's raining! It's pouring! You press your nose to the window and watch the raindrops zigzag down the pane. It looks as if the rain will never stop. But don't be glum. Perk up a rainy day with a tea party!

For decorations, you can hang lightning bolts right over the table. But the only clouds at this party will be the ones you eat on—cloud place mats—and the ones you eat up—cloud cookies.

Rain, rain, *don't* go away!

LEMON DRIZZLE CAKE

You will need:
A juicer
1 large lemon

3 tablespoons sugar
1 pound cake

Squeeze the lemon and stir the sugar into the juice. (Don't use the seeds!) Mix well. Set aside for 15 minutes. With a fork, poke lots of deep holes in the top of the pound cake. Drizzle the sweet lemon juice over the cake. Serve sliced. (You can cut cookie cutter shapes from the slices.)

CLOUD COOKIES

Did you ever wonder what a cloud might taste like? Try these cookies. Ask an adult to help.

You will need:
A glass bowl   *½ teaspoon vanilla*
2 egg whites   *½ cup sugar*

1. Preheat the oven to 250°.
2. Beat egg whites and vanilla until foamy. (Use a glass bowl.) Beat in sugar, one tablespoon at a time, until very stiff and shiny. (You can gently fold in some chocolate chips if you like.)
3. Line a cookie sheet with foil. Drop batter by teaspoonfuls 2 inches apart. Bake one hour. Cool for 30 minutes.

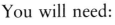 Makes 48 cookies.

MUD PIES

You will need: *¾ cup confectioners' sugar*
⅓ cup unsweetened cocoa   *¼ cup cream cheese, softened*

Stir cocoa, sugar, and cream cheese together until smooth. Chill in refrigerator for 1 hour or more. Shape teaspoonsfuls of the mixture into little pies. Refrigerate until you're ready to serve.

Spicy drinks are perfect for wet, cold days. For a wonderful Rainy-Day Tea, try orange spice or apple cinnamon tea. Or serve hot apple juice and cinnamon. Turn to page 2 for tea-making directions and more ideas.

LIGHTNING BOLTS

You will need: *Yellow colored paper*   *String*   *Tape*

Cut three lightning bolts out of the colored paper. Tape a piece of string to each one and ask an adult to help you hang them over the table.

CLOUD PLACE MATS

You will need: *White and gray colored paper*

Cut the colored paper into a cloud shape. Make one for yourself and one for each guest.

When you're all ready, pass the Lemon Drizzle Cake. Then serve the Cloud Cookies and the Mud Pies.

Mmmmm. Why doesn't it rain more often?